NATIONAL
GEOGRAPHIC

Bird Beaks

Emily Ballinger

This bird's beak is long and thin.
This bird drinks nectar with its beak.

hummingbird

This bird's beak is **short** and **sharp**.
This bird cracks seeds with its beak.

parrot

This bird's beak is **flat** and **wide**.
This bird catches fish with its beak.

spoonbill

This bird's beak is **curved** and **thick**.
This bird catches fish with its beak.

puffin

This bird's beak is **large** and **strong**.
This bird picks fruit with its beak.

toucan

This bird's beak is tiny and pointed.
This bird catches bugs with its beak.

wren